Mastering the Pixel 9a

A Complete Guide to Setup, Customization, and Daily Use

Bella Smarty

Disclaimer

This independent guide was created solely for educational and informational purposes to assist users in understanding and operating their Pixel 9a smartphone more effectively. It is not affiliated with, endorsed by, or sponsored by Google LLC or any of its subsidiaries.

All trademarks, brand names, logos, and product references used within this book remain the property of their respective owners. Any mention of such names is made purely for descriptive and reference purposes to identify the product accurately and does not imply any association or endorsement.

The content is based on publicly accessible information, general usage, and the author's understanding of the device at the time of writing. While reasonable efforts have been made to ensure accuracy, the author and publisher accept no responsibility for errors, omissions, or outcomes resulting from the application of this material.

This publication does not attempt to promote, market, or sell any specific hardware, software, or service. For official instructions, support, and updates, readers should consult the manufacturer's documentation or customer service.

Table of Contents

Introduction

Welcome to Your Pixel 9a

Congratulations on your new Pixel 9a! This guide was created to help you tap into everything your smartphone has to offer — from setup to customization, from camera tips to advanced features that make everyday tasks easier and more enjoyable.

Are you transitioning from another phone or exploring this device for the first time? You'll find straightforward steps, helpful insights, and time-saving tricks throughout this book. Each chapter is written to walk you through the essentials with clarity — no technical jargon, no fluff — begin exploring your device with confidence

Inside, you'll learn how to personalize your device, navigate its most powerful tools, and fix common hiccups along the way. From setting up your home screen and securing your data, to discovering clever shortcuts and using the built-in voice assistant effectively — everything you need is right here.

By the time you've reached the final page, your Pixel 9a won't just be a new phone —it'll feel like a natural extension of your day-to-day routine. Let's get started and make the most of your new device.

Overview of Key Features

The Pixel 9a is more than just a sleek smartphone — it's designed to make everyday life smoother, smarter, and more enjoyable. From its vibrant display to intelligent photography features and responsive performance, this device brings together powerful tools in one streamlined package.

Here's a look at the standout features that make this phone a true companion for both productivity and play:

📸 Smart Camera System

Capture crisp, colorful photos in nearly any environment with the Pixel 9a's dual-camera setup. The main lens produces detailed images with rich contrast, while the wide-angle lens allows you to fit more into the frame — perfect for landscapes or group shots. Built-in photo processing enhances low-light shots, reduces blur, and brings out natural tones without needing filters or editing apps.

Vibrant pOLED Display

The phone's 6.3-inch pOLED screen delivers bold colors, deep blacks, and smooth motion. Whether you're scrolling through photos, watching videos, or reading on the go, the display remains fluid and sharp thanks to its adaptive refresh rate of up to 120Hz. It's designed to be responsive in bright daylight and gentle on the eyes at night.

⚡ Powerful Custom Processor

Inside the Pixel 9a is a high-performance chip designed to handle everything from multitasking to mobile gaming with ease. The processor ensures apps launch quickly, run smoothly, and conserve power when possible — so your experience stays fast without draining the battery.

🔋 All-Day Battery Life

With a robust 5,100mAh battery, you can go from morning to night without needing a midday recharge. And when it's time to top up, fast-charging support makes powering up quick and convenient. Wireless charging is also available for added flexibility.

🔐 Security and Smarts, Built-In

From fingerprint unlocking to facial recognition, the Pixel 9a offers quick, secure access to your device. It also includes built-in privacy controls, app permission settings, and automatic system updates to help keep your information protected and your phone running smoothly over time.

🌐 Lightning-Fast Connectivity

With support for next-gen network speeds, the Pixel 9a keeps you connected in real-time — whether you're video calling, streaming content, or uploading large files on the move. Wi-Fi and Bluetooth pair seamlessly with your other devices, and hotspot sharing is built right in. Together, these features create a phone that's flexible, powerful, and intuitive — ready to adapt to your routine and help you do more with ease.

Getting to Know Your Pixel 9a's Design

Before diving into features and customization, it's helpful to get familiar with the physical layout of your Pixel 9a. Knowing where everything is makes navigation easier and helps you take full advantage of what your device offers.

■ Front of the Device

Dominating the front is a 6.3-inch pOLED display that stretches nearly edge to edge, offering an immersive viewing experience. At the top of the screen sits the front-facing camera, ideal for video calls and quick selfies. The bezels are slim, giving the phone a modern, clean appearance while maximizing screen space.

You'll also find front-facing speakers built into the top bezel — delivering clear audio whether you're watching a video, making a call, or listening to music.

■ Right Side: Power and Volume

On the right edge of the phone, you'll find two key controls:

- **Power Button**: This is used to turn your phone on or off and wake or lock the screen. It also houses the fingerprint sensor — a fast, secure way to unlock your device with just a touch.

- **Volume Buttons**: Located just below the power button, these allow you to quickly adjust media volume, ringer levels, and in-call sound. They also serve as shutter controls when using the camera app.

■ Left Side: SIM Tray

The left edge is home to the SIM tray, where you can insert a physical SIM card. The device also supports eSIM technology, allowing you to activate mobile service digitally if your carrier supports it — no physical card needed.

■ Top of the Phone

At the top, you'll find a microphone that helps capture ambient sound and improves clarity during calls and voice recordings. It works alongside other mics on the device to reduce background noise.

▼ Bottom Edge: Charging and Audio

You'll find the following along the bottom of the phone:

- **USB-C Port**: Used for charging your phone and transferring data. It's compatible with fast-charging adapters and supports connection to accessories like headphones or USB drives (with the appropriate adapter).

- **Speaker and Microphones**: A second speaker and additional microphones sit here as well, working with the top speaker to produce stereo sound and enhance voice clarity.

■ Back of the Device

Flip the phone over, and you'll find the rear camera module in the upper left corner. It houses the main and ultrawide lenses, along with a flash. The rear surface is smooth, with a subtle logo positioned toward the center for a clean, minimal look.

Taking a few moments to get familiar with your phone's layout sets the stage for confident, easy use. Whether you're snapping a photo, adjusting sound, or charging up — everything you need is right at your fingertips.

Getting Started

Unboxing and Setup

Before you dive into your phone's features, it's important to set things up smoothly and securely. This chapter walks you through those first few steps — from unboxing to connecting and personalizing your device.

⬢ What's in the Box and How to Get Started

Once you've opened your new Pixel 9a, you'll find the phone itself, a USB-C charging cable, a SIM ejector tool, and a small setup guide. To power up, press and hold the button on the right side until the screen lights up.

You'll be greeted with a simple step-by-step walkthrough. Start by choosing your language and region, then adjust accessibility options if needed.

Switching from another phone? You'll have the option to transfer data using a cable or wirelessly — a convenient way to bring your apps, contacts, and messages over in one go.

The process is straightforward, and once complete, your phone will begin to take shape around your preferences.

🌐 Connecting Online and Syncing Your Info

Next, choose a Wi-Fi network and enter the password to get online. This connection allows the phone to check for software updates and begin syncing content linked to your account — like backups, photos, emails, and apps.

If you don't have an account yet, you'll have the option to create one during this process. From there, your phone will begin restoring settings and personal data that help make the experience feel familiar and tailored to you.

🔒 Locking Things Down: Security Made Simple

Security is a major part of setup — and it doesn't have to be complicated. You'll first be asked to choose a screen lock method: a PIN, pattern, or password. This becomes the base layer of protection for your phone.

From there, you can add a fingerprint for faster unlocking. Simply tap your finger on the power button sensor as prompted until the scan is complete.

Do you want to unlock your phone just by looking at it? Facial recognition is available too. It uses the front camera to create a secure profile of your face, which works better in perfect lighting.

By the time you finish this step, your phone will be not just personalized but protected.

Customizing Your Device

Personalizing Your Pixel 9a

Now that your phone is set up and secure, it's time to make it feel like your own. This chapter walks you through how to customize the look, sound, and feel of your Pixel 9a—from layout changes to notification controls and display tweaks that fit your preferences.

Home Screen Layout and Widgets

Your home screen is your daily command center — so it should reflect your style and habits.

To rearrange app icons, tap and hold any icon, then drag it to a new location or folder. You can remove icons from the home screen without uninstalling the app by dragging them toward the top of the screen until "Remove" appears.

Want to check the weather, calendar, or reminders at a glance? Long-press anywhere on the home screen, tap "Widgets," and explore options like clocks, to-do lists, and quick access tiles. You can drag, resize, and rearrange them to create a space that works for you.

🔔 Managing Alerts: Notifications and Sound Settings

Notifications don't need to interrupt your day — they should serve you.

Go to **Settings > Notifications** to control how alerts behave. You can mute certain apps, allow priority messages only, or schedule "Do Not Disturb" for quiet hours. You'll also find sound controls under **Settings > Sound & Vibration**, where you can adjust ringtone volume, vibration intensity, and system sounds.

You can even set different ringtones for different contacts — perfect for knowing who's calling before you look at the screen.

🌙Display Settings: Brightness, Font Size, and Dark Theme

Your screen can adapt to your needs — visually and practically.

Under **Settings > Display**, you'll find controls to adjust brightness manually or enable adaptive brightness, which automatically responds to your lighting environment.

Want easier reading? Tap **Display size and text** to increase font or icon size — ideal if you prefer larger visuals. There's also a setting for bold text if you want a bit more contrast.

Many users also enjoy enabling **Dark Theme**, which swaps bright backgrounds for darker tones. It's easier on the eyes in low light and may help extend battery life. You can turn it on manually or schedule it to activate at specific times — like sunset to sunrise.

By customizing these visual and audio elements, your phone becomes more than a device — it becomes your digital comfort zone, built around how you see, hear, and interact with the world.

Exploring the Pixel 9a

Features That Make It Shine

Beyond the basics, the Pixel 9a comes with some powerful tools that elevate how you capture, communicate, and control your day-to-day. In this section, we'll explore the camera system, the built-in voice assistant, and the deeper settings that help fine-tune your experience.

■ Capturing the Moment: Camera Tips and Editing Tools

The Pixel 9a's camera system is built for simplicity and performance — no fancy gear needed. You'll find two lenses on the back: one for detailed everyday shots and another for wide-angle photos that fit more into the frame.

Open the Camera app and swipe through different modes like Portrait, Night Sight, and Video. Want to zoom? Use two fingers to pinch or double-tap the screen. For low light, the night mode automatically boosts clarity without using flash.

After snapping your shot, tap the image preview in the corner to open the editor. Here, you can adjust brightness, crop, sharpen, or apply filters. These built-in tools are intuitive, letting you polish photos quickly without leaving the app.

Whether you're capturing a sunset, a quick selfie, or a close-up of something you need to remember — the Pixel 9a makes it effortless.

🎤 Hands-Free Help: Using the Built-In Assistant

Your phone comes with a smart assistant that can answer questions, set reminders, check the weather, and even send texts — all by voice. To activate it, say the wake phrase (it begins with "Hey...") or press and hold the power button for a second.

You can ask it to:

- Set a timer.

- Play a song.

- Navigate somewhere.

- Send a message.

- Call a contact.

- Translate a phrase.

You can even use it to control smart home devices or check your calendar. It learns your voice over time for better results, and it works whether your screen is locked or open — as long as settings allow.

To adjust what the assistant can do, go to **Settings > System > Gestures or Voice Input**, and customize permissions to your liking.

⚙ Tuning the Experience: Advanced Settings at a Glance

Want to explore the deeper layers of your device? Head into **Settings**, where you'll find tools to fine-tune behavior, performance, and preferences.

Some useful areas to explore are:

- **System Gestures**: Customize how the phone responds to swipes, taps, or button combinations.

- **Digital Wellbeing**: Track screen time, set app limits, and schedule focus time to avoid distractions.

- **App Management**: Review what's running in the background and control permissions.

- **Security and Privacy**: View recent activity and app access, and adjust permissions by category.

These tools are designed to give you control without overwhelming you. You don't have to change everything at once — just knowing where to look is the first step toward making the phone work the way you want.

Battery Performance and Charging Options

Your Battery in Your Control

Your Pixel 9a is built to keep going through busy days and long hours — but knowing how to manage its battery and charging options can make a big difference. This chapter walks you through smart ways to make the most of every charge, from simple optimizations to advanced power-saving tools.

⚡ Getting the Most from Your Battery

With its 5,100mAh battery, the Pixel 9a offers solid all-day performance. Still, usage patterns — like screen time, brightness levels, and background activity — can affect how long a single charge lasts.

Here's how to make your battery go further:

- **Adjust Screen Brightness**: Lowering brightness or enabling adaptive brightness helps reduce power drain.

- **Limit Background Activity**: Go to **Settings > Battery > Battery Usage** to see which apps are using the most power. You can restrict apps that run unnecessarily in the background.

- **Turn Off Unused Features**: If you're not using Bluetooth, location services, or mobile hotspot, turning them off can stretch your battery life noticeably.

These small tweaks can lead to big gains — especially if you're away from a charger for a while.

🔌 Charging Options: Wired and Wireless

The Pixel 9a supports both wired and wireless charging, giving you flexibility based on what's available.

- **Wired Charging**: Use the included USB-C cable and a compatible fast-charging adapter to get a quick boost — around 50% in just 30 minutes, depending on the charger.

- **Wireless Charging**: Simply place your phone on a Qi-compatible charging pad. While it charges more slowly than wired methods, it's ideal for overnight or desk use.

You can view battery status and charging speed right on the lock screen or in the notification shade.

⬛ Power Saver Features

When you're on the go and your battery starts running low, your phone offers built-in tools to help it last longer:

- **Battery Saver**: This feature limits background activity, turns off visual effects, and pauses some services to reduce power usage. Turn it on manually or set it to activate automatically when the battery hits a certain percentage.

- **Extreme Battery Saver**: Found under **Settings > Battery**, this tool limits your phone to only essential apps and functions. It's ideal for emergencies or travel days when charging might not be an option.

These tools are easy to activate and highly customizable — you decide which apps remain active in extreme mode.

Even if you are a light user or constantly on the move, your Pixel 9a offers the tools to stretch every charge and keep you connected longer.

Apps and Storage Management

Managing Your Apps and Storage

Your Pixel 9a gives you the freedom to install, organize, and back up apps and data however you like. Whether you're a minimalist or an app enthusiast, this chapter shows you how to stay in control of everything that lives on your device — without clutter or confusion.

🧹 Installing and Organizing Your Apps

To download apps, open the default app store and search for what you need. Tap "Install," and the app will appear on your home screen or in the app drawer automatically.

Want to keep things neat? You can:

- **Create folders** by dragging one app icon over another.

- **Remove icons** from the home screen without uninstalling them.

- **Rearrange apps** by long-pressing and dragging to your preferred location.

If you're unsure which apps are safe or popular, look for high-rated reviews and "Editor's Choice" tags to help guide your selection.

For those who like a clean layout, you can also hide or disable pre-installed apps you don't use. Just go to **Settings > Apps**, tap on the app, and select **Disable** or **Uninstall**, depending on what's allowed.

■ Checking and Managing Storage

Over time, apps, downloads, and media can eat up space. To stay ahead of storage issues:

- Visit **Settings > Storage** to see a visual breakdown of what's taking up space.

- Use the **Smart Storage** tool to automatically clear backed-up photos or large files you haven't opened in a while.

- Clear cache and unused data from individual apps via **Settings > Apps > [App Name] > Storage & cache.**

You can also move photos and videos to cloud storage to free up space while still keeping your memories accessible.

☁ Backing Up Your Data

To protect your information in case of loss or upgrade, automatic backup options are built in.

Go to **Settings > System > Backup**, and ensure that backup is turned on. This will save:

- App data and settings

- Call history and text messages

- Device preferences

- Photos (if linked to cloud storage)

You can view when the last backup occurred and manually trigger a new one if needed. If you're ever switching to another device in the future, restoring from this backup will make the transition feel seamless.

Keeping your phone tidy and your data safe doesn't have to be a chore. With a few smart habits, you'll always have space for what matters — and peace of mind knowing your information is backed up.

Staying Connected

Everyday Features That Just Work

Your Pixel 9a is more than a smart device — it's a connection hub that helps you stay in touch, share files, and get things done efficiently. This chapter walks you through essential tools for communication, sharing, and staying online wherever you are.

📡 Wi-Fi, Bluetooth, and Mobile Data Made Simple

Getting online is as simple as a few taps.

- **Wi-Fi**: Go to **Settings > Network & internet > Wi-Fi**, choose your network, and enter the password. Once connected, your phone will automatically rejoin the same network next time.

- **Mobile Data**: If you're using a SIM or eSIM plan, mobile data will likely be active by default. You can turn it on/off in **Quick Settings** or under **Mobile**

Network in the main settings menu.

- **Bluetooth**: For pairing wireless earbuds, speakers, or smartwatches, head to **Settings > Connected devices > Bluetooth**. Make sure Bluetooth is enabled, tap "Pair new device," and select from the list.

Need to toggle these quickly? Swipe down twice from the top of your screen to access the Quick Settings panel — perfect for turning things on and off on the go.

📞 Calls, Messages, and Email: Staying in Touch

Your phone makes communication seamless and flexible.

- **Calls**: Use the default dialer app to make calls, block spam, access voicemail, or see recent contacts. You can even screen unknown callers with built-in call filtering.

- **Messages**: The messaging app supports both standard texts and advanced messaging features — like read receipts and high-quality image sharing — when connected to Wi-Fi or data.

- **Email**: Set up your email account(s) by opening the pre-installed mail app and signing in. Most major providers like Gmail, Outlook, and Yahoo are supported, and additional apps can be downloaded if you prefer another interface.

You can also add multiple email addresses to the same app, allowing you to check personal and work accounts from one place.

→▊ Sharing Files Instantly with Nearby Share

Need to send photos, links, or documents to someone nearby without cables or apps? Your device's built-in Nearby Share makes it easy.

- Open the file or item you want to share.

- Tap the **Share** icon and select **Nearby Share.**

- Make sure Bluetooth and location services are on.

- The other person's device will appear once it's visible and ready to accept.

Nearby Share uses a combination of Bluetooth, Wi-Fi, and peer-to-peer communication to deliver content quickly — no internet connection required.

Troubleshooting Tip: If Nearby Share doesn't detect the other device, ensure both devices have visibility enabled and that you're within close range.

No matter how you connect — through data, wireless accessories, or real-time conversations — your Pixel 9a is designed to make every interaction feel seamless.

Troubleshooting and Support Tips

Resolving Common Issues

Even the most reliable devices run into the occasional hiccup. Whether an app freezes, your phone slows down, or something just doesn't seem right, this chapter will help you get back on track — quickly and confidently.

▲ Resolving Common Issues

If something feels off — like the screen lagging, buttons not responding, or apps not opening—don't panic. A few quick actions usually solve the problem:

- **Restart your phone**: Press and hold the power button, then tap "Restart." This clears temporary bugs and refreshes memory.

- **Close background apps**: Swipe up from the bottom, hold, then swipe away unused apps.

- **Check for updates**: Go to **Settings > System > System update** and install the latest version available. Updates often contain important bug fixes.

Small issues are often resolved with one of these simple steps — no tech support required.

■ Handling App Crashes and Slow Performance

Sometimes an app will misbehave — crashing, freezing, or refusing to open. Here's what you can do:

- Go to **Settings > Apps**, select the app, and tap **Force stop**, then **Clear cache**.

- If that doesn't help, try **Clear storage** — but note that this may reset the app's data.

- You can also uninstall and reinstall the app if the problem persists.

If the overall system feels sluggish, consider checking your storage usage under **Settings >**

Storage or reducing animations under **Settings > Accessibility > Remove animations**.

■ Reset and Recovery Options (If Things Get Serious)

If a major issue arises — such as your phone refusing to turn on or system-wide glitches that won't go away — you might consider a full reset. But this step should always be a last resort.

To reset safely:

- Go to **Settings > System > Reset options.**
  .
- Choose **Erase all data (factory reset)**

- Follow the on-screen prompts and confirm when ready.

⚠ **Important**: This will delete all personal data, so always back up your device first via **Settings > System > Backup**.

A factory reset restores your phone to its original state, which can be useful if you're preparing to sell or give away the device — or need a clean slate to fix recurring problems.

With a few practical steps and the right settings, you can resolve most common problems on your own — no tech expertise required. Your Pixel 9a is built to bounce back fast when things go wrong.

Keeping It Secure

Privacy, Updates, and Everyday Care

Your Pixel 9a is more than just a phone — it holds your messages, memories, and personal data. This chapter helps you keep everything protected, up-to-date, and running smoothly for the long haul.

🎥 Privacy Settings and App Permissions

One of the most important habits for digital safety is managing what your apps can access.

Go to **Settings > Privacy** to explore options like

- **Permission Manager**: See which apps have access to your location, microphone, camera, contacts, and more. Revoke or grant access as needed.

- **Notifications**: Decide which apps can interrupt you — and which can stay silent.

- **Personal Data Usage**: Control how much diagnostic or usage info is shared, and opt out of personalized ads or tracking features.

For even more control, visit **Settings > Security & privacy > App security**, where you'll find alerts for any suspicious activity or newly installed apps.

These tools are simple to use but powerful in maintaining your peace of mind.

■ Keeping Your Phone Updated

Software updates don't just bring new features — they also fix bugs and improve security.

To check for updates:

- Go to **Settings > System > System update.**

- Tap "Check for updates" and follow prompts if an update is available.

Your device is designed to check for updates automatically, but it's smart to run a manual check occasionally — especially if something feels off or outdated.

Updating regularly helps your phone stay fast, safe, and compatible with the latest apps.

● Long-Term Care: Cleaning and Maintenance Tips

A little maintenance goes a long way in keeping your device in top shape:

- **Clean your screen and ports** regularly with a soft, lint-free cloth.

- **Use a case and screen protector** to avoid wear and tear.

- **Avoid overheating** by keeping your phone out of direct sunlight for extended periods.

- **Restart your phone weekly** to refresh system memory and close background processes.

You can also monitor overall performance under **Settings > Device care** or **Battery**, where you'll see tips on optimizing usage and extending lifespan.

With a few simple habits and occasional check-ins, your phone will continue to feel just as smooth and secure as the day you turned it on.

Advanced Tips and Hidden Features

Getting More from Your Pixel 9a

Now that you've explored the setup, features, and tools that make your Pixel 9a a powerful everyday companion, it's time to unlock even more. This final chapter shares practical shortcuts, lesser-known features, and a few expert tips to help you squeeze every last drop of value from your phone.

⏱ Time-Saving Tricks That Make a Big Difference

Here are a few small changes that create a smoother experience:

- **Quick App Switching**: Swipe up from the bottom and pause to see recently used apps. Swipe sideways to jump between them instantly.

- **One-Handed Mode**: Shrink the screen for easier reach by enabling one-handed mode in **Settings > System > Gestures**.

- **Quick Screenshot**: Press the **Power** and **Volume Down** buttons together to capture your screen.

- **Tap to Wake**: Double-tap the screen to wake the device without pressing the power button.

These features become second nature quickly — and once you've used them, it's hard to go back.

🌑 Discover Hidden Features

Some of the most useful tools are the ones you won't notice at first:

- **Live Caption**: Automatically adds subtitles to any video or audio, perfect for quiet environments. Find it under **Accessibility settings**.

- **App Suggestions**: On the home screen, suggested apps will appear based on time of day and usage habits. You can turn these on/off under **Home Settings**.

- **Digital Wellbeing**: Want to unplug more often? Set app limits or schedule "focus time" to avoid distractions throughout the day.

- **Smart Storage**: Automatically removes backed-up photos and videos to save space without losing anything important.

These tools are designed to adapt quietly in the background — giving you more freedom and fewer interruptions.

By now, you've done more than just set up a smartphone —you've created a device that fits your habits, protects your data, and helps you stay connected and productive. Whether you're exploring creative features, keeping up with work, or just staying in touch with those who matter most, your Pixel 9a is ready to support you every step of the way.

Technology should feel personal — and now it does.